TABLE OF CONTENTS   PAGE

1. **OPENING THOUGHTS**   2

2. **PROFITING FROM BUSINESS**   5
    - Greg's Lemonade Stand   8
    - Jessica's Lemonade Stand   10
    - Amanda's Babysitting Service   13
    - Flipping/Retail Arbitrage   18
    - Other Income Streams   19
    - Section Review   21

3. **FINANCIAL ASSETS & RISK**   22
    - History of Money   25
    - Stocks   26
    - Fixed Income   29
    - Currencies   30
    - Commodities   31
    - Real Estate   32
    - Risk   33
    - Section Review   35

4. **ECONOMICS THAT MATTER**   36
    - Introduction   37
    - Supply vs. Demand   39
    - Business Cycle   40
    - Interest Rates   41
    - Inflation & Deflation   42
    - Asset Returns with Inflation   43
    - Section Review   44

5. **PERSONAL FINANCES**   45
    - Compounding Returns   46
    - Credit Cards   50
    - Cash Flow   51
    - Spending   53
    - Needs vs. Wants   54
    - Power 5 Spending Principles   56
    - FICO   57
    - Section Review   59

6. **FINAL THOUGHTS & RESOURCES**   60

7. **GLOSSARY (references)**   64

OPENING THOUGHTS

Ask any two people what Financial Literacy means and we are confident you will likely get mixed responses. We might have an understanding as adults, yet no one has figured out how to explain this material properly to the younger generations.

The average American does not know enough about Financial Literacy. That leads to further financial problems during the span of their lives, and the lives of their families as well.

Financial Literacy is about making smart decisions with your money. As that happens, you will become more confident about managing your money. No matter who you are or what you do, we all have to manage our finances. An absolute critical life skill.

We are going to teach you the language and the simple math involved. The earlier you learn this, the greater understanding and foundation you will build, in regard to personal finance. Our goal is to help you become much smarter than the average American (at any age), when it comes to handling your money.

Trust us, life is much more enjoyable when your money is working for you. Here are some alarming facts:

- TOO MANY AMERICANS LIVE PAYCHECK TO PAYCHECK
- TOO MANY AMERICANS DO NOT HAVE AN EMERGENCY FUND
- TOO MANY AMERICANS CARRY EXPENSIVE CREDIT CARD DEBT

We are here to help the younger generation form a better money plan to live their best life.

Our approach to teaching you about Financial Literacy is also different. We want you to have the right skill sets for success with your finances.

With that in mind, we are teaching you the following:

1. **HOW A SIMPLE BUSINESS CREATES PROFIT?**

    Why? So you can generate profits for yourself.

2. **THE MAJOR FINANCIAL ASSETS & THE CONCEPT OF RISK?**

    Why? So you can build your personal wealth.

3. **ECONOMICS THAT MATTER.**

    Why? Money is a tool. Economics is the study of human behaviors & teaches you about limited resource management.

4. **PERSONAL FINANCE**

    Why? Here we cover the most important aspects of cash management. You will learn the crucial habits and foundation concepts for long term money success.

5. **GLOSSARY OF TERMS/CONCEPTS**

    Why? To help with your reinforcement and to provide a reference section.

6. **CLOSING THOUGHTS**

    Why? A fun section explaining your potential and the mindset and the mindset needed to win the long game of life.

    This is simple. It is doable.

    Follow along as we teach you one page at a time.

    READY?

    Turn the page to learn how income is created by businesses.

SECTION TWO

PROFITING FROM BUSINESS

BUSINESS SECTION

Here's the deal. We are going to show you how a business makes its profits. Whether a company sells a product or service, the math will be the same.

Maybe it's the digital wallets or it's the simplicity of buying on Amazon. Culturally, we have moved away from paper money. Getting paid in paper money just hits differently. It's immediate. You can feel it.

Your financial development has been limited by digital money.

Have you earned any money for yourself yet?

We need to make sure that you really understand how to generate income.

As you generate more income, personal finance becomes much easier to manage. We are all about positive cash flow. The more the better.

You have every right to make money in America. Never, ever, apologize for being financially successful.

This is where Financial Literacy needs to begin. Teaching young adults how to generate income for themselves. This is how your situation will begin to change for the better.

We are excited to show you how a business generates income. You are more than capable of picking up on this process. The math isn't complicated at all and neither is the language.

We want to share a quick secret about our approach. We treat everyone with respect and as a capable person. We do not care about your age!

Trust us to teach you the key income fundamentals.
Trust us to make the material age appropriate.
WE GOT YOU.

All businesses need to be profitable to survive. If a business begins to lose customers or to lose money, their days will be numbered.

A successful business can afford to pay employees. That salary helps workers afford to live their lives. We all need to earn a salary or income to cover our personal bills and lifestyle.

Every business needs customers to support their product or service.

Customers can be retail, corporate or government.

Now, we are going to show you how some simple businesses earn their profits.

Net profits are what matters.

That is what you keep after expenses.

GREG'S LEMONADE STAND

The classic lemonade stand. Old as time. It is the "gateway" to business ownership. You might have tried running one. You probably have bought from a local stand at some point in your life.

You will be amazed at the numbers behind a lemonade stand. It is a perfect simple business to start analyzing. LET'S DO THIS.

Costs: What Greg purchased to make sales.

Greg buys powdered lemonade online. He paid $4 to make 20 cups to sell.

He plans to sell his lemonade for 50 cents per glass.

Greg is going to work the stand 2 hours in the morning and 2 hours in the afternoon.

Morning Sales Activity:

Customer 1 pays 50 cents for a glass
Customer 2 pays $1 for 2 glasses.
Customer 3 pays $1 for 1 glass
Customer 4 pays $3 for 4 glasses

Afternoon Sales Activity:

Customer 5 pays $1 for 1 glass
Customer 6 pays 75 cents for 1 glass
Customer 7 pays $2 for 3 glasses
Customer 8 pays $3 for 4 glasses
Customer 9 pays $1 for 2 glasses
Customer 10 pays $1 for 1 glass

The $14.25 at the bottom?
That's **GROSS profit.**

Money collected from his customers.

Gross Profit doesn't include expenses.

Gregs Lemonade Stand		
	Paid	Glass Count
Cust 1	$ 0.50	1
Cust 2	$ 1.00	2
Cust 3	$ 1.00	1
Cust 4	$ 3.00	4
Cust 5	$ 1.00	1
Cust 6	$ 0.75	1
Cust 7	$ 2.00	3
Cust 8	$ 3.00	4
Cust 9	$ 1.00	2
Cust 10	$ 1.00	1
	$ 14.25	

GREG'S LEMONADE STAND

Now let's factor in the costs (also called expenses).

Greg spent $4 to make 20 glasses of lemonade. He had to spend that money in order to sell the lemonade. His mom gave him red plastic cups. The water came from the fridge filter.

Greg has spent $4 to be able to run the stand. If he doesn't make any sales, he will be out that amount. The expenses related to producing a product or service are called **"Cost of Goods Sold" or "COGS"**.

Now, please take a look at the excel sheet below. We have added the costs on the right side **(in red)**. We can now solve for Net Profit.

Gross Profit - Costs (COGS) = Net Profit

$14.25 - $4.00 = $10.25

Gregs Lemonade Stand			COGS per glass = $4 /20 units or (0.20)			
Customers	Paid	Units Sold	COGS	x Units		Net Profit per customer
Morning:						
Customer 1	$ 0.50	1	$ (0.20)	$ (0.20)		$ 0.30
Customer 2	$ 1.00	2	$ (0.20)	$ (0.40)		$ 0.60
Customer 3	$ 1.00	1	$ (0.20)	$ (0.20)		$ 0.80
Customer 4	$ 3.00	4	$ (0.20)	$ (0.80)		$ 2.20
Afternoon:						
Customer 5	$ 1.00	1	$ (0.20)	$ (0.20)		$ 0.80
Customer 6	$ 0.75	1	$ (0.20)	$ (0.20)		$ 0.55
Customer 7	$ 2.00	3	$ (0.20)	$ (0.60)		$ 1.40
Customer 8	$ 3.00	4	$ (0.20)	$ (0.80)		$ 2.20
Customer 9	$ 1.00	2	$ (0.20)	$ (0.40)		$ 0.60
Customer 10	$ 1.00	1	$ (0.20)	$ (0.20)		$ 0.80
Gross Profit	$ 14.25	20	Costs	$ (4.00)		
Net Profit = Gross Profit - Costs				$ 10.25		$ 10.25

Net Profits are real profits because they include COGS.

Greg earned $10.25 as Net Profit over the entire day running his Lemonade stand.

He keeps that amount because Net Profit includes COGS

JESSICA'S LEMONADE STAND

Jessica's friend Heather is having a big garage sale. Jessica wants to sell lemonade there because she knows there will be good customer traffic at this spot.

She convinces Heather to let her sell lemonade, but Jessica has to split 25% of the profits with her friend.

Should Jessica split gross profits or net profits with Heather?

Jessica should split net profits with Heather because net profits always include expenses. If Jessica splits the gross profits, then she will be paying all the costs herself. That is not how you set up a business to make money.

What are Jessica's expenses or COGS?

      Lemonade: Liquid from a big box. She paid $36 to make 120 cups.

      Plastic cups: She paid $6 for 120 red cups.

      Teaching point: Do you see that the COGS is -$42 to sell 120 cups?

      How much is that per cup if she sells all 120?
      Answer: -$42/120 = .35 cents

Jessica plans to charge .75 cents per glass.

She hopes most customers will not ask for any change back.

Heather's family is advertising the garage sale so that will help. They are selling toys, clothes, tools, & household items. Plus, the weather is great!

HERE WE GO!

JESSICA'S LEMONADE STAND

Ten cars pull up before the garage sale opens. Jessica will be busy today.

The first group of customers buy 20 glasses of lemonade at the average price of $1. That is $20 gross profit.

The second group of customers buys 10 glasses of lemonade for $15. That is $15 gross profit.

It is super crowded now. The weather is really helping business. The third group buys 17 glasses of lemonade for a $21 gross profit.

Most customers aren't asking for change either. The first 3 groups bought 47 glasses of lemonade for $56 gross profit. (green)

Jessica's Lemonade Stand			
What	Cost	Count	Per Glass
Lemonade	$ (36.00)	120	-0.3000
Red Cups	$ (6.00)	120	-0.0500
Total Costs	$ (42.00)	120	-0.3500
Charging	.75 per glass of lemonade		
Customer Groups	Glasses Sold	Avg Price	Gross Profit
1st Group	20	$ 1.00	$ 20.00
2nd Group	10	$ 1.50	$ 15.00
3rd Group	17	$ 1.24	$ 21.00
	47	1.19	$ 56.00

We know that Jessica has spent $42 on COGS to sell the lemonade.
She has earned +$56 in Gross Profit after 47 customers.
She has now covered Costs and is currently +$14 of Gross Profit

JESSICA'S LEMONADE STAND

Here is how the rest of the day went for Jessica:

The 4th group of customers bought 25 glasses of lemonade for $35.

The 5th group of customers bought 30 glasses of lemonade for $37.50.

The final group bought 18 glasses of lemonade at the average price of $1.75 per glass. That would be $21 of gross profit for the 6th group.

Jessica's Lemonade Stand Final Figures: 120 glasses sold			
What	Cost	Count	Per Glass
Lemonade	$ (36.00)	120	-0.3000
Red Cups	$ (6.00)	120	-0.0500
Total Costs	$ (42.00)	120	-0.3500
Charging	.75 per glass of lemonade		
Customer Groups	Glasses Sold	Avg Price	Gross Profit
1st Group	20	$ 1.00	$ 20.00
2nd Group	10	$ 1.50	$ 15.00
3rd Group	17	$ 1.24	$ 21.00
4th Group	25	$ 1.40	$ 35.00
5th Group	30	$ 1.25	$ 37.50
Final Group	18	$ 1.75	$ 21.00
	120	$ 1.25	$ 149.50

Jessica's Lemonade Stand Final Figures	
Gross Profit	$ 149.50
Average Gross Profit Per Glass	$ 1.25
Costs:	$ (42.00)
Net Profit	$ 107.50
Average Net Profit Per Glass	$ 0.90
Profit Split with Heather -25% Net Profits	$ (26.88)
Jessica's Profits Post Split	$ 80.63
Jessica's Profit Per Glass	$ 0.67

Summary: Gross profit $149.50
Net profit $107.50

Per Glass: Gross $1.25
COGS -.35 cents
Net +.90 cents per unit

Profit split with Heather (right in green): Splitting net profit of $107.50

Jessica (+75%) keeps $80.63
Heather (+25%) collects $26.88

AMANDA / BABYSITTER

Amanda is a great babysitter. She charges $20 per hour when she sits.

She normally sits 2 nights a week working with three families. Each booking averages 3 hours each time. She knows eight families that want her help. Her friends are also great sitters.

Amanda plays softball in the spring. She can only work 1 night per week now with her new sports schedule. WHAT'S A GIRL TO DO?

Amanda has averaged +$120 a week over the last 6 weeks. She is averaging 6 hours a week of sitting. She is saving money for a used car. She is looking for a creative solution. DO YOU SEE IT?

Amanda - As Sitter

Families	Week 1	Week 2	Week 3	Week 4	Week 5	Week 6	Total
Brown	60	60		60		60	240
Rosenbergs		60	60		60		180
Smith	60		60	60	60	60	300
	120	120	120	120	120	120	720

Amanda had 8 families that wanted her help. She has the friends to do the sitting.

She figures it out. She can book the sitting appointments and have her friends help out. Keeping it simple, let's just say that the families are cool with it and so are her friends. This is called "**sub-contracting**."

Amanda will charge the families $20, give her friends $15 per hour and she will keep the $5 per hour for herself for booking the sitters.

AMANDA / BABYSITTER

Teaching Point:

How many hours will Amanda need to book as a "subcontractor" to recover the $60 deficit per week because of hew new spring softball Schedule?

Answer: She will be making $5 per hour for any work she schedules for her friends.

$60 / $5 = 12. She needs to book 12 hours of work for her friends.

Can Amanda make that happen? LET'S FIND OUT!

WEEK ONE:

Sitter	Family	Sitting	Scheduling	Amanda	Friends	Total
Amanda - Sitting and Scheduling First Week of New Schedule						
Amanda	Smith	3		60	0	60
Jill	Brown		2	10	30	40
Isabella	Rosenbergs		4	20	60	80
Corey	Chaplins (new)		3	15	45	60
Erin	Miller (new)		2	10	30	40
		3	11	115	165	280

Analysis:

Amanda worked 3 hours and scheduled 11 hours for her friends. Amanda was -$5 short of her weekly goal.

Not a bad first week, at all!

14

AMANDA / BABYSITTER

WEEK TWO:

Sitter	Family	Sitting	Scheduling	Amanda	Friends	Total
Amanda - Sitting and Scheduling Second Week of New Schedule						
Amanda	Smith	3		60	0	60
Jill	Brown		2	10	30	40
Isabella	Rosenbergs		3	15	45	60
Corey	Chaplins (new)		3	15	45	60
Erin	Miller (new)		2	10	30	40
Neil	Jones (new)		2	10	30	40
		3	12	120	180	300

Analysis:

Amanda was able to book 12 hours and work 3 hours. She met her weekly target of $120.

WEEK THREE:

Sitter	Family	Sitting	Scheduling	Amanda	Friends	Total
Amanda - Sitting and Scheduling Third Week of New Schedule						
Amanda	Smith	2		40	0	40
Jill	Brown		3	15	45	60
Isabella	Rosenbergs		2	10	30	40
Corey	Chaplins (new)		2	10	30	40
Erin	Miller (new)		4	20	60	80
Neil	Jones (new)		3	15	45	60
Christie	Thomas (new)		3	15	45	60
		2	17	125	255	380

Amanda	Sitter	SC Friends	Total	(+/-)
Week 1	60	55	115	-5
Week 2	60	60	120	0
Week 3	40	85	125	5
Totals	160	200	360	0
Weekly Average		3	120	

Analysis:

Amanda books 17 hours for her friends. She only works 2 hours this week as a sitter. She made +$125 for the week. She is also back to averaging +$120 per week through 3 weeks (section on right).

AMANDA / BABYSITTER

WEEK FOUR:

Amanda - Sitting and Scheduling Fourth Week of New Schedule						
Sitter	Family	Sitting	Scheduling	Amanda	Friends	Total
Amanda	Smith	4		80	0	80
Isabella	Rosenbergs		2	10	30	40
Corey	Chaplins (new)		2	10	30	40
Erin	Miller (new)		4	20	60	80
Neil	Jones (new)		3	15	45	60
Christie	Thomas (new)		3	15	45	60
		4	14	150	210	360

Amanda	Sitter	SC Friends	Total	vs. Target
Week 1	60	55	115	-5
Week 2	60	60	120	0
Week 3	40	85	125	5
Week 4	80	70	150	30
Totals	240	270	510	30
Weekly Average		4	127.5	

Analysis:

Amanda sat for 4 hours this week and scheduled 14 hours for her friends. This was her best week so far, +$30 vs. her $120 target. Her weekly average also jumped to $128 (+$8).

WEEK FIVE

Amanda - Sitting and Scheduling Fifth Week of New Schedule						
Sitter	Family	Sitting	Scheduling	Amanda	Friends	Total
Amanda	Smith	2		40	0	40
Isabella	Rosenbergs		2	10	30	40
Corey	Chaplins (new)		4	20	60	80
Erin	Miller (new)		2	10	30	40
Neil	Jones (new)		3	15	45	60
Christie	Thomas (new)		2	10	30	40
Jill	Brown		2	10	30	40
		2	15	115	225	340

Amanda	Sitter	SC Friends	Total	vs. Target
Week 1	60	55	115	-5
Week 2	60	60	120	0
Week 3	40	85	125	5
Week 4	80	70	150	30
Week 5	40	75	115	-5
Totals	280	345	625	25
Weekly Average		5	125	

Analysis:

This week, Amanda is short -$5, as she only made +115. She is doing well managing her sitting service. Through 5 weeks she is now averaging +$125 per week (see right section).

AMANDA / BABYSITTER

WEEK SIX

Amanda - Sitting and Scheduling Sixth Week of New Schedule						
Sitter	Family	Sitting	Scheduling	Amanda	Friends	Total
Amanda	Smith	3		60	0	60
Isabella	Rosenbergs		3	15	45	60
Corey	Chaplins (new)		2	10	30	40
Erin	Miller (new)		4	20	60	80
Neil	Jones (new)		2	10	30	40
Christie	Thomas (new)		4	20	60	80
Jill	Brown		3	15	45	60
		3	18	150	270	420

Amanda	Sitter	SC Friends	Total	vs. Target
Week 1	60	55	115	-5
Week 2	60	60	120	0
Week 3	40	85	125	5
Week 4	80	70	150	30
Week 5	40	75	115	-5
Week 6	60	90	150	30
Totals	340	435	775	55
Weekly Average		6	129.2	

Analysis:

Amanda finished strong in her last week making +$150. She sat for 3 hours herself and booked 18 hours for her friends. Amanda now understands how to properly scale her business. She was able to earn $90 completely from subcontracting.

Final Review:

Amanda did a fantastic job of looking ahead, managing her schedule and beating her weekly goal of $120 per week. The excel on the top right shows the weekly breakdown.

She averaged more money per week than if she was just sitting by herself (+$9). She either met or beat her weekly goal of $120, 4 out of the 6 weeks.

Amanda was also creative enough to figure out a way to keep earning, despite her busier spring schedule. That's the power of subcontracting a business.

This is a cool way of showing you how to solve a problem, doing some light forecasting and then showing her progression.

FLIPPING / RETAIL ARBITRAGE

We encourage all young adults to try flipping.

It works because the big box stores want to move their merchandise at scale. Their margins (profit per item) are already locked and loaded before putting their goods out to sale.

Certain products become very popular on Amazon, eBay, or even locally (Facebook Marketplace) for sale. That increased demand can cause the internet price to greatly exceed the retail price from the big box stores.

Flippers can profit on the pricing difference between the big stores and the online retailers (arbitrage).

There are 3 steps to flipping:

     1) Source the product (Walmart, Target, Cosco)
     2) List the product online (Amazon, eBay, Facebook)
     3) Ship the product to the paying customer

I have done it (Coach Bloom). I plan on doing it again at some point. It's an excellent way to increase monthly income.

     Example: Bluetooth Speakers
          $15 at Walmart (on clearance)
          List on eBay for $55
          Customer buys it for $50
          Shipping costs $5

          $50 minus COGS (1$20) = $30 profit

Do this 30 times a month and you could earn +$900

OTHER INCOME STREAMS

GIG ECONOMY WORK

These are temporary work positions. You do them for a specific period of time. Most often not real careers. Gig work does not come with any benefits, such as healthcare or a 401k match.

You are paid per job, ride or hour.

      Pros: Flexible hours. You can stack extra income.

      Cons: Lack of benefits and not a long term solution.

      Examples: Uber, Doordash, Fiverr, Instacart

E-COMMERCE

Involves the buying or selling of anything over the internet. Doesn't matter if it's through your phone or laptop. Instead of working a job here, you are setting up a store or building a brand.

      Pros: It's scalable. Your business is always available 24/7 which is cool. Someone may buy this course while we sleeping. HECK YEAH!

      Cons: You only get paid on sales made. You do not truly know if or when your idea will work. Unpredictable.

      Examples: E-books, E-courses, dropshipping, online stores.

OTHER INCOME STREAMS

The next two alternative sources are for the big dreamers out there. Go ahead and try, but please know the odds are probably not in your favor.

All of the performance-based careers are insanely competitive.

Be young and follow your dreams. Everyone finds their level at some point. TRUST US, WE KNOW THIS TO BE A FACT.

ESPORTS

If you are a top Esports gamer you can earn a pretty good monthly income of $5k to $20k. If your team wins a tournament, you share in the winnings.

Beyond the players, this is a huge ecosystem. You have owners and manager roles out there. Huge business opportunities on this side of it, regarding advertising and league management.

We like where Esports is going. It may be a bit hard on the gaming side but there are plenty of more consistent roles on the management side.

SOCIAL MEDIA INFLUENCERS

This is the dream, right? Get your followers up and the money comes to you. Has anyone told you how yet?

Go and do something super cool in the real world that makes you famous. Come back to social media afterwards. Monetize it. Easier said than done.

Influencing is real, you can make money. If you are not famous then you should have an area of knowledge that people come to you for online. Tutoring, tech lessons, flipping, writing, etc. Find your niche and go for it.

PROFITING FROM BUSINESS / REVIEW

By teaching you how a business works, we have established what NET Profit looks like. That is also positive cash flow in personal finance (Chapter 5).

You should now be able to set up your own small business to make a profit.

You will need to make more revenue than your expenses. If you want to pay staff, then you need to make even more net revenue to cover those salaries as well.

We didn't just stop at a basic lemonade stand.

Jessica's lemonade stand included a profit split with Heather. Cool stuff.

Amanda's babysitting service had some forecasting involved. She was able to make her friends some money and keep the rest for herself.
THAT IS A BIG WIN-WIN.

I also wanted to explain the alternative income streams:

    Flipping is an excellent choice for young adults to earn side money.

    The Gig economy can help you earn extra money in the short term.

    Building an E-commerce store or brand makes sense. We just wouldn't count on it as your main income. It does have the potential to scale well.

    Esports has a huge ecosystem, as gaming is very competitive.

    Social media influencing also looks tough, but is very possible over time.

FINANCIAL ASSETS & RISK

This is an important chapter towards your financial literacy success. Owning financial assets will help you build more wealth over your lifetime. You just need to learn just about the assets you will one day be acquiring,

The goal here is to increase your awareness and understanding of the 5 major financial asset groups. We also want you to understand how market risk really works.

In the first chapter, we covered how a simple business makes their income. That is important so you will be able to generate enough personal income to cover your expenses. We will discuss the lifestyle/cash management portion regarding spending, in chapter 5.

We want to get you invested in the markets as soon as possible because an early start allows your money to compound and grow faster. More time also reduces risk.

When you are bringing in good income and your spending is under control, you are then ready for investing.

Positive cash flow is always a MUST before investing.

So what is an asset?
An asset is anything of VALUE that you OWN. If an asset is being financed, then it isn't being fully owned by you.

For example: You can finance a house, a car, or a smartphone. They are assets of course, but you do not truly own them until they are paid off.

FINANCIAL ASSETS AND RISK

Financial assets are also fully owned by you. There are 5 major asset groups you need to know. Once purchased, they become a part of your personal portfolio or holdings.

Most of the time, when we hear about financial assets, people just assume it's only the stock market. That is ok, but not entirely accurate.

Other major asset groups which the average person is not aware of:

- The fixed income and currency markets are considerably larger in terms of their money value.

- We have the real estate market, which impacts the value of houses and office buildings.

- There is also a large commodity market that allows farmers and others to trade their produce/harvests.

We will get into all of these other financial assets. But first, let's do a very short history lesson about why money needed to be created in society.

FINANCIAL ASSETS / HISTORY OF MONEY

Money in either physical or digital form is accepted because it is a:

- **means to exchange items**
- **measurement of wealth**
- **way to store profit or wealth**
- **method to buy or sell goods or services**

What happened before this magical thing called money existed?

THOSE POOR SOULS HAD TO BARTER.
They had to trade livestock or tools for maybe
clothing or whatever else they needed but didn't
have on them.

They had to agree on the value of each side of the
exchange of goods vs. goods. No deal was completed
until both sides agreed on the exchange.

Bartering just took too long. The transaction speed was way too slow.

Something was needed to speed up transaction times and to create a smoother way to either buy or sell, rather than simply exchange.

Money became the net difference.
Trading begins in its earliest form.

It did not matter whether the money was a
stone, a coin or even paper.

What mattered was that they agreed on its value.
Which they did.

Money becomes the first financial asset, like EVER!

Officially, the Greeks are credited with forming the first official government coin.
ENOUGH ABOUT MONEY, LET'S MOVE ON!

FINANCIAL ASSETS / STOCKS

STOCKS AND THE STOCK MARKET

STOCKS: You can own an amount of stock in public companies that are listed on exchanges. The amount of stock is called shares. If you like the product or service and believe the company will continue to grow, then you might want to become an investor. Stocks are also called equities. Own enough stock and you could have some voting rights.

Stocks are easily the most popular financial asset with the general public.

Think Amazon, Google, Apple, Starbucks, Tesla, Pepsi. These types of companies.

ETFs: EXCHANGE TRADED FUNDS. Similar to stocks, you can trade ETFs In the stock market. They can be a basket of stocks a sector, a Country, or region. They track most assets. ETFs do not have to hold stocks. They trade at one price, based on their holdings during the day.

You now have the ability to own fractional shares. This is a huge development for young people. You can now buy an amount of stock or ETF that you can afford. This means you can start with less money. You can learn quicker. This is relatively new. It allows the masses to have partial ownership of a stock for a dollar value that they can afford.

Combining ETF's with FSO's (fractional share ownership) is a big time advantage. No other generation has ever been able to begin investing with very little start up money. WE ENCOURAGE YOU TO START TODAY!

FINANCIAL ASSETS / STOCKS

An example of fractional stock ownership:

    1 share of Tesla (TSLA) costs $1001.00

    Before FSO, it would cost you at least that much to own a share.

    With FSO, you can now buy $100, $200, $500 or any amount you want to purchase of TSLA.

    Want to buy Tesla monthly, with little money. Now you can.

STOCK TYPES

DIVIDEND STOCKS: These stocks distribute some of their earnings back to shareholders. These dividends are paid on a schedule (monthly, quarterly, or semi-annual). The dividend rate changes as the stock moves in price. You are capturing income from a stock here. Examples are T, JNJ, MCD. BMY. Look them up and see.

AT&T is a dividend stock. It pays 5.5% of earnings, every 90 days, back to its shareholders.

AT&T (T)

McDonalds (MCD)

FINANCIAL ASSETS / STOCKS

Growth stocks are expected to "outgrow" the average stock. We expect a higher return on our growth stocks. They have a higher valuation, which means they are more expensive than your average stock. You are paying more for the expected higher return. Most growth stocks in 2020 are in the technology sector.
Examples are TSLA, ZOOM, PYPL, AMZN, NFLX.

Tesla (TSLA) has always been expensive relative to its fundamentals. This year really captured its growth potential.

TSLA returned +247% in 2020

QQQ returned +24% in 2020

TSLA beat the NASDAQ by +223% in 2020

Value stocks have been pushed by the market. They have a low valuation (opposite of growth). They are considered cheap.

These stocks are in out of favor sectors like banking, energy or restaurants (2020).

Stocks with a large physical footprint continue to be punished,
Examples are JPM, WMT, XOM

FINANCIAL ASSETS / FIXED INCOME

FIXED INCOME MARKETS

These markets are where loans take place. Corporations and governments can issue debt (loans) to fund new projects. There is a schedule of repayment back from the corporation or government to the bond (debt) holder. Not only will the amount of the debt be paid back at the end, but there is also usually an amount of interest collected too.

Corporations borrow money to fund new products/projects to expand potential revenue sources. Governments borrow money to fund schools, parks, stadiums, etc.

When it comes to credit, the more financially responsible the corporation or government is, then the more likely you will get your money back. They get a lower rate because of that. A lower rate means less interest paid by the issuer. The buyer receives lower interest as well.

Better credit = better/lower rates (cheaper financing).
Corporations and all levels of government are rewarded for good credit.

You are also rewarded for good credit in personal finance.

Government bond types:

- Treasury - Federal
- Municipal - State and local government

Corporate Bond Types

- Secured and unsecured - It's secured if backed by an asset
- Senior to Junior - Ranking of preference
- High Yield - Credit rating not strong or potentially junk
- Convertible - Can become a stock

FINANCIAL ASSETS / CURRENCIES

CURRENCY MARKETS

Open 24/7. One of the bigger asset classes around the globe.

In the United States we have the dollar, in Europe they have the Euro and Great Britain has the pound.

Currencies do not gain value on their own like stocks. They gain or lose value in relation to other currencies. That is because they are being exchanged for each other continuously.

Fiat currency is backed by a county. They exist as long as that country stays in power. Our US $ is a great example.

Bitcoin is a digital currency. It is not Fiat currency. It is not backed by any country. This is a new currency form, so it will be volatile until it becomes more mainstream. THIS IS HAPPENING NOW!

We have included our entire Digital Assets guide to the back of this course. That is how much growth has occurred during the last 3 years.

Corporations use the currency market to bring home money they earn in a foreign country.

Central banks of large governments use the currency market to set policy and in some instances support their currency.

The US $ is the world's reserve currency for now. We are trusted that we will pay back all our obligations and our strong military helps.

Did you know that global oil is settled in the US $?

FINANCIAL ASSETS / COMMODITIES

COMMODITY MARKETS

A commodity is a basic good used in commerce that is interchangeable with other like kinds. Commodities are most often used as inputs in the production of other goods and services.

The quality of a given commodity may differ slightly, but it is essentially uniform across all producers.

There are two main types of commodities. Hard and soft.

Soft commodities are produced by farmers and ranchers. They are grown above the ground.

        Examples: Coffee, wheat, sugar, corn, beef, chicken, oranges and grapes

Hard commodities come from the earth. There are a finite or limited amount of these resources.

        Examples: Diamonds, gold, silver, coal, oil, rubber and natural gas

Water and time are also a commodity. They are both considered precious, yet we don't trade them. It is important to be aware of that.

Before electronics and technology took over the physical pits for trading, Chicago and London were the major trading venues for global commodities.

FINANCIAL ASSETS / REAL ESTATE

REAL ESTATE MARKET

Real estate is property made up of land and usually buildings. This can be residential, which is meant for families to live on. It can also be commercial, where businesses operate from. This includes any rights above or below ground.

The real estate market will always depend on location.

Residential properties (homes) will always care about the educational quality and amount of taxes.

Commercial or industrial properties will be more concerned with the local population and the price of the land.

Residential

Commercial

The real estate asset class is normally a rate sensitive market. That is because most properties are financed from the fixed income markets. Homes can be paid fully in cash, but most people are not able to do so.

There is a big industry around real estate.

- Construction - The building of new residential, commercial, or government buildings.

- Agents - Helping buyers or sellers of properties.

- Investments - You can buy a home or property to sell (flip). You can also buy a property to rent out (rentals).

REAL ESTATE IS A VERY IMPORTANT ASSET CLASS. WE LOVE THAT CASH FLOW.

FINANCIAL ASSETS / ABOUT RISK

One of the biggest blind spots in financial literacy is the lack of understanding about financial risk.

What does risk mean in life?
Exposing something or someone to danger or harm. It is considered a negative. But we all know you need to take risks sometimes in life to be rewarded.

Life example:	If you are a new skier, you should stick to the green slopes. Trying a double diamond would be very risky or dangerous. You could get seriously injured. Not worth the risk.

What does financial risk really look like?
It is the probability of either a gain or loss on your financial asset position. You could either be rewarded or punished by the market. Outcomes are not guaranteed. The uncertainty about achieving your investment objectives is the risk you take on as an investor.

The biggest difference about investment risk is that the market can also reward you. When in life, it is usually considered a negative.

Financial assets trade at a given price daily. Markets tend to gain value over time. You want to stay in markets as long as possible.

Trading is generally riskier than investing. Traders are more price sensitive than investors. They buy and sell over shorter time frames.

Traders < 2 years					Investors > 2 years

Time is on the side of the investor because markets want to go higher longer term. Since 2008 we have stimulated the markets higher to create wealth for owners of most financial assets.

FINANCIAL ASSETS / RISK CONT'D

Technical analysis is the study of price using charts. It is very effective for risk management. I encourage all new traders or investors to learn technical analysis for making their buy/sell decisions. It is very important to have a plan versus just trying to time the markets with a roll of the die.

There is an old saying about risk. Never forget this one.

"The return OF your assets is always more important than the return ON your assets".

Your gains or losses are "unrealized" until you sell your assets. Those gains or losses only count once they are "realized" or sold.

Financial assets to follow in the markets:

EQUITIES
- Apple (AAPL)
- Amazon (AMZN)
- S&P 500 ETF (SPY)

FIXED INCOME
- 7-10 yr bond (IEF)
- 20+ yr bond (TLT)
- High yield (HYG)

COMMODITIES
- Gold (GLD)
- Oil (USO)
- Agriculture (DBA)

CURRENCY
- Yen/USD (FXY)
- USD Index (UUP)
- Euro/USD (FXE)

REAL ESTATE
- US market (VNQ)
- Homebuilders (XHB)
- REITs (SCHH)

FINANCIAL ASSETS / REVIEW

Time is on your side as a young adult. This section was about raising your awareness of financial assets and the important concept of financial risk.

Once your personal finances are in order, you can begin your journey as an investor.

The 5 major financial asset groups are:

1. **Stocks**
2. **Fixed Income**
3. **Real Estate**
4. **Commodities**
5. **Currencies**

Digital Assets have arrived. Soon we will consider Crypto as the 6th Asset Class.

Money in either coin or paper form was the OG financial asset.

Financial assets trade at an agreed upon price. Not all financial assets are guaranteed. Prices can change for many reasons.

Risk means that you might make or lose money on an investment or business decision.

Investing is important to creating long-term wealth.
Investing is how you grow your wealth.

If you liked learning about financial assets, then you should start following them on a weekly basis. Keep a short list of stocks and ETFs to monitor. Create a Yahoo finance account. It is free.

Finally, know that price is truth. Price is the news. The story comes after.

SECTION FOUR

ECONOMICS THAT MATTER

ECONOMICS / INTRO

Economics is the study of how human beings or societies make decisions using their limited resources. From those limited resources they can create, distribute or consume among other groups (trade).

Money is also a limited resource that can be applied to creating, building or spending on other goods and services.

Modern economics theory began with Adam Smith who wrote "An Inquiry Into the Nature and Causes of the Wealth of Nations" way back in 1776. Yeah, that was quite a long time ago.

Microeconomics

The focus is on individuals:

- A single person
- Families and Households
- Businesses
- From the bottom up

Macroeconomics

The focus in on larger groups:

- Towns, states, countries
- Regional - Continents
- Demographic groups
- From the top down

ECONOMICS / MICRO

Price is the cost charged to purchase a good or service.

Price is also where you can buy or sell financial assets.

But…do you know what determines the price you are paying?

SUPPLY vs. DEMAND — This sets the price you are paying. Price is always determined by market forces. The level of demand is offset by the amount of that product (Supply).

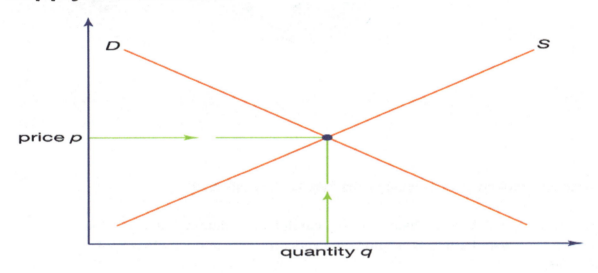

© 2013 Encyclopædia Britannica, Inc.

The relationship of supply vs. demand is as old as time. It will always set the price paid. It works for all goods and services regardless of the point of sale.

Quantity is the amount of a product made.

Demand is the popularity of a given product at a certain price.

That is how supply vs. demand works. Just like our lemonade stand example in the income section.

Should we expect to sell lemonade at $5 or is it more realistic to sell it at .50 cents?

SUPPLY vs. DEMAND EXAMPLE

BEANIE BABIES

PHOTO: PAT CARROLL/NY DAILY NEWS ARCHIVE/GETTY

These little stuffed animals were all the rage back in the 1990's.

The company which made them was very careful about limiting supply to the stores. They were hard to find, and some versions were impossible to find on purpose.

The limited supply drove demand to very high levels. It became a frenzy or mania. These stuffed animals became very expensive due to the limited supply.

This is a real-life example of supply vs. demand. The limited supply drove the prices much higher.

Have you ever noticed the limited supply impacting the price on something that you have wanted to buy?

We bet you can think of a few things!!

ECONOMICS / MACRO

At the macro level, we can analyze the performance of larger groups. Countries release economic data and statistics on a regular basis. These are measured for activity.

Economic business cycles have four phases, they are:

EXPANSION: +Employment +Growth +Price Measures

PEAK: Top of the cycle.
+Full employment +Max Growth +Price Inflation

CONTRACTION: -Employment -Growth -Price Measures

TROUGH: Bottom of the business cycle.
Employment stabilizes, growth no longer goes down and settles in.

Graph 1

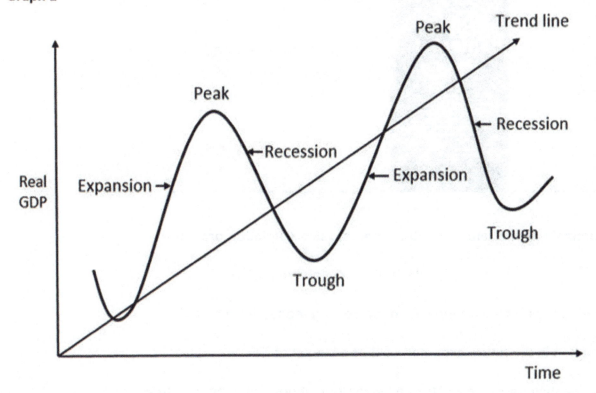

Note:
The above is a normal business cycle. Please know that if a government provides stimulus, it is possible to extend the expansion or to limit the contraction phases.

ECONOMICS / INTEREST RATES

Nominal interest rates are what the banks or financing companies charge their customers to take out a loan. These loans originate from the fixed income markets.

We discussed fixed income in the financial assets section.
Do you remember that fixed income is a major asset class?

When we borrow money from a bank, we expect to pay both the principal and interest back before the loan matures.

When banks lend us money to finance an asset, they are including inflation in the financing rate. Inflation is the future price expectation of goods and services.

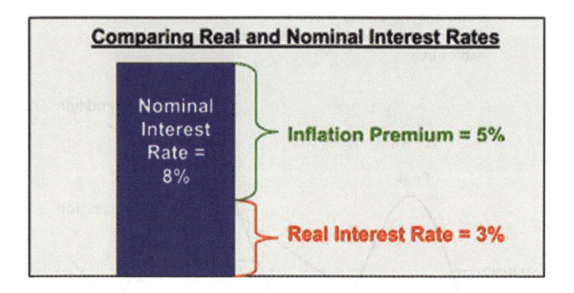

Nominal interest rates =   Real interest rates + inflation premium

8% = 3% + 5% (above picture)

Real interest rates are the cost of borrowing money from a bank.

Inflation is the future expected cost of a basket of goods.

On the next page, we will take a closer look at how inflation is actually calculated.

ECONOMICS / INFLATION and DEFLATION

THE BURGER INDEX (Inflation Example)

Below we have the identical burger at two distinct points in time.
Over ten years, the burger's price has risen by $1.05 to $4.11 (2005-2015).
That is an increase of 34% over a span of a decade. We could also say that the yearly inflation rate was 3.4% (34%/10 yrs).

2005
$3.06

2015
$4.11

vs

INFLATION vs. DEFLATION

The average price level of goods and services can fluctuate up and down. The burger example showed inflation because the price had increased over time.

Normally prices do increase over time. That is why nominal interest rates will always include inflation (prior page).

Deflation happens when the average price level fluctuates lower (down) between two time periods. Deflation occurs in the present.

Consumers slow down their spending.

We can expect lower prices for food, cars and even financial assets. When this happens, consumers will wait as long as possible to delay purchases in a deflationary environment.

Make sense?

ECONOMICS / ASSET RETURNS

A successful economy needs to continue growing.
Inflation will naturally occur in most growing economies.

One day in the future, you will become an investor. For that to happen, your personal finances have to first be in good shape. You will learn all about cash management in the personal finance section.

Let's presume you are ready to be an investor.

Would you agree that future goods or services will become more expensive in the future due to inflation?

We would want our financial asset returns to also beat inflation over the long run. The average person does not understand how inflation lowers their overall asset returns. See below.

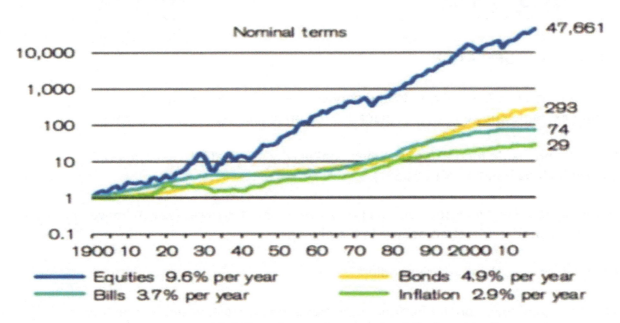

Inflation is a major, silent wealth killer. It remains a major blindspot to the average person. We are so proud to explain this to you properly.

As the chart shows, a +2.9% inflation rate, with your equities returning +9.6% a year, would actually only be worth +6.7%.

In this case, our future money has been weakened by inflation.

ECONOMICS / REVIEW

Economics was my major in college. It was ok but I cannot say it was fun or super exciting.

As an adult though, it totally makes much more sense. We see it everywhere and see its application multiple times a day.

We all know that price matters. It is what we pay for things. It is what we pay for financial assets as well.

We now know that if demand goes up, then price may follow higher.

If demand goes down, the price should follow lower (cheaper).

Too much supply of an item that is not seeing demand, then we can expect lower prices.

Too little supply of an item that isn't seeing demand, then we can expect higher prices.

There is also a business cycle in economics. Expansions and recessions are just phases in a cycle. We do not want to overreact to either of them,

Inflation matters.
It means that prices are going up.

The interest rates we pay on loans have inflation built into the rate. For long term wealth, your savings/investments will also have to beat inflation.

Inflation weakens your future money because everything is now more expensive.

Deflation is also dangerous.
Prices can crash lower.

Technology is deflationary. But it is not healthy for economic growth. You do not want to make major purchases during deflationary phases because you do not know when it will end.

SECTION FIVE
PERSONAL FINANCE

PERSONAL FINANCE

Financial literacy is about making the best decisions you can with your money.

Young adults in high school and college do not need to focus fully on insurance, taxes or managing their investments just yet.

We do want to focus on generating income and we also want to focus on how we spend that income. We can also benefit by applying the best habits and a simple approach to your financial success. Especially because time is on your side as a young adult.

We have built you skillsets up to this point, so that you are now ready to fully comprehend this section. You should be confident applying everything we were able to discuss and cover.

You are more than capable of generating income even at your age. That's why we started with business income first. Those concepts are valuable here too.

In the third chapter, we raised your awareness of the major asset groups and the concept of risk. We have to get our cash management in shape before we begin investing. That increases the amount of time you give yourself before investing.

Now we are going to show you why controlling your personal cash flow is so important. Making income increases your cash flow position. Spending that income decreases your cash flow position. We can invest in ourselves much faster with a positive monthly cash flow.

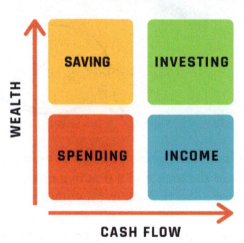

Check out the matrix that we created.

Positive cash flow is the fuel to your money.

How you spend it determines your miles per gallon.

You want to be efficient.

Increasing your cash flow gives you the ability to begin investing and building your wealth.

PERSONAL FINANCE / COMPOUNDING

COMPOUNDING RETURNS

This is your motivation for controlling your spending. As a young adult you have so much time on your side. Everyone will tell you to invest as early as possible.

What they will not tell you is that you need two components to achieve compounding returns for life.

1. **You need the market risk to reward you with a positive return on your financial assets.**

2. **You also need to leave your investments alone over time. The magic of compounding does take some time. You cannot treat your investments like an ATM (automated teller machine).**
EARLY SELLING ISN'T AN OPTION.

We do not have full control over market risk. Longer time frames will normally help risk assets grow better.

We do have full control over our personal finances and most importantly, how we spend that income. Positive cash flow gives you an emergency savings account.

Positive cash flow gives you more room for life to happen. Things will come up. With a cash balance and a positive cash flow, you will not need credit cards and you will not need to cash in on your investments.

Now that we know why, let us go over compounding returns. Yes, it is a financial concept. It is a life skills concept as well.

PERSONAL FINANCE / COMPOUNDING

COMPOUNDING RETURNS (cont)

Albert Einstein famously said that compound interest is the most powerful force in the universe, "compound interest is the 8th wonder of the world".

Compounding returns can also be called compound interest, it's the same concept. **I like using compounding returns because it better describes the reward of focused effort over time. The concept transcends money fyi.**

CR or CI means: Earning interest on your money balance that was previously earned as just interest. That increases your principal balance each year. It is financial momentum. Look at the 20 year example below.

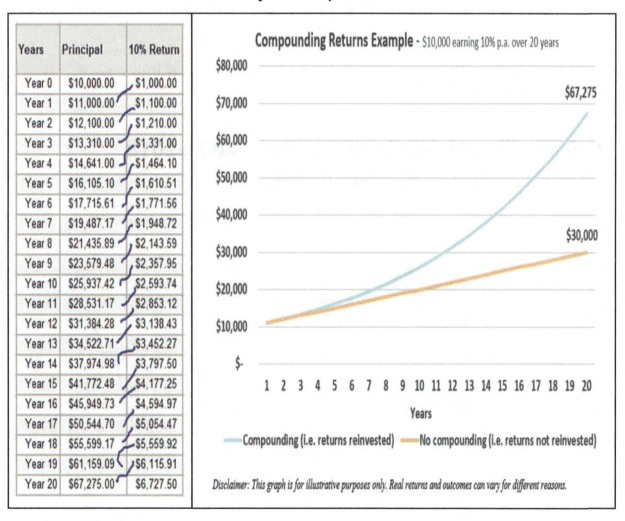

Now that we know why, let's go over compounding returns. Yes, it is a financial concept. It is a life skills concept as well.

PERSONAL FINANCE / COMPOUNDING

OK, so we want compounding interest to work for us on our own investments. We want it to earn as much as possible. Anywhere we can.

We do not want to PAY compounding interest. Yet, the average American does just that by carrying unpaid credit card balances.

The language is misleading on purpose. Unpaid credit cards lead to debt. That CC debt is VERY expensive (rates charged).

Those unpaid debt balances compound against you every month until paid off.

UNDERSTANDING PERSONAL CASH FLOW WILL HELP YOU AVOID MAJOR CREDIT CARD DEBT.

Credit cards are a predatory financial product. The average American now carries over $10k of CC debt. We are going to show you how harmful they truly are. They are also a major wealth killer.

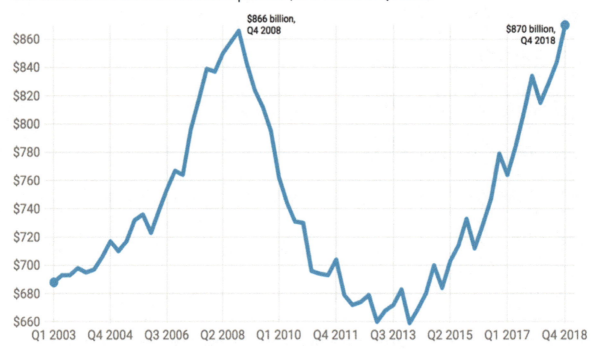

PERSONAL FINANCE / CREDIT CARDS

The average credit card rate is now -15% per year on unpaid credit card balances (see chart).

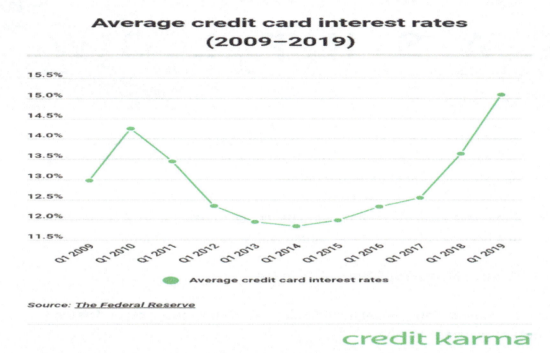

Now, imagine you bought something expensive with a credit card, but you are unable to pay the entire amount. You are just making the minimum payments.

Example: You spend $9000 on furniture you cannot afford.

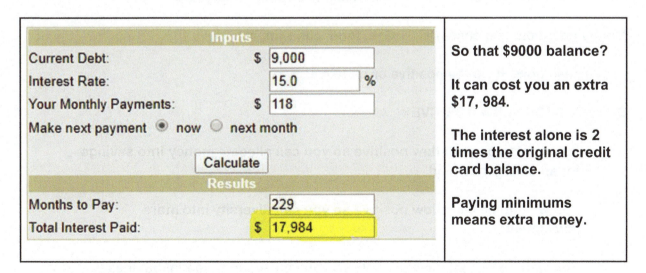

So that $9000 balance?

It can cost you an extra $17, 984.

The interest alone is 2 times the original credit card balance.

Paying minimums means extra money.

By not paying off the furniture right away, the total cost over time went from $9000 to $27000. Total cost became 3 times as expensive.

PERSONAL FINANCE / CASH FLOW

We can now finally discuss one of the most misunderstood personal finance concepts. If the average person understood cash flow properly, we wouldn't have as much credit card debt outstanding per person.

We also wouldn't have as many people living paycheck to paycheck. It is the main reason why this financial literacy course began with a business section.

BUSINESS NET INCOME = PERSONAL CASH FLOW

Getting personal finance right is not as difficult as you think, once you understand how businesses generate income.

Cash Flow: Just like a business, you need to know your personal finances from head to toe. Where is the money coming IN from versus the money going OUT.

Money coming in (income) = Paycheck, allowance, salary, etc.

Money going out (expenses) = Gas, food, car, rent, etc.

That's cash flow. It can be positive or negative.

SO WHY CASH FLOW POSITIVE?

> You want to be cash flow positive so you can allocate money into savings for an emergency fund.
>
> You want to be cash flow positive so you can diversify into more investments.
>
> You want to be cash flow positive so you can act on potential business ideas.

PERSONAL FINANCE / CASH FLOW

Positive cash flow creates financial strength.

Your monthly income exceeds your monthly expenses. It creates money to allocate towards a stronger tomorrow for yourself.

Use it for savings. Use it for investments. Use it to build a business.

You will not be counting on your next paycheck to cover today's bills. It buys future time, choices and freedom.

Example: Jim is cash flow positive. He earns $5000 per month.
        He spends -$4000 per month. He has +$1000 to save/invest each month.

Negative cash flow creates financial weakness.
Your monthly expenses exceed your monthly income. This causes most Americans to live paycheck to paycheck. They are spending money ahead of schedule, most likely with credit cards. There is then no money left to save or invest.

Negative cash flow can be fixed.
Either increase your income or lower your expenses. It also adds to financial and emotional stress. It kills future time, opportunity and choice.

Example: Karen is cash flow negative. She earns $3000 per month.
        She spends -$3500 per month. She has no money to save/invest.

        Most likely the $500 per month she is short will become credit card debt.
        That will compound at -15% against Karen per year. Karen is making her
        life more complicated.

        She is the average American living paycheck to paycheck.

PERSONAL FINANCE / SPENDING

We know from economics that money can be a scarce commodity. You will be paid income based on the value you bring to your company. You can earn income based on how profitable your business becomes.

You can increase income by working a 2nd job.

I hope your skill sets will generate above average income. Some of you will exceed the average income. Some of you will start below the average income. The good news is that you now understand how to improve or add income.
IT DOES NOT HAVE TO COME FROM JUST 1 SOURCE. THOSE DAYS ARE OVER.

With personal finance, it is not what you make, it is what you keep.

We can control how we spend our money, where or what we spend our money on. We should spend our money in areas that contribute to our personal happiness. We could also spend money to improve our skill sets to improve future income.

Positive cash flow is the objective. Spending controls make sure you get there as soon as possible. **Again, it is what you keep.**

From an early age, we are taught to be consumers. Buying "that" car will make you cool. "This" outfit will make you happy. "The" new makeup will make you even prettier. YOU GET THE IDEA.

It is time for some money reprogramming. It is not your responsibility to keep the economy going by spending all of your money every paycheck.

Every dollar you spend is a vote supporting that company which makes whatever product or service you are purchasing. But you must..

Vote for yourself, take care of yourself before the others (bills).

PERSONAL FINANCE / SPENDING

There is zero compromising on needs. They are essential to daily life. You must have a bed, food and clothing.

NEEDS VS. WANTS

A need is something thought to be a necessity or essential items required for life

Examples of needs:
- Food
- Water
- Shelter

A want is something unnecessary but desired or items which increase the quality of living

Examples of wants:
- Car stereo
- MP3 player
- Designer clothes

Wants would be great to have. Wants could make your life more enjoyable. They are not as essential to your daily life. Controlling your emotional purchases of wants, is really the key to personal finance.

You can have most of what you want today, you just can't have EVERYTHING you want today. Simply put, leave some of your money for tomorrow. I know that it is a challenge because we live in an instant gratification culture. You might think you need it now. But In reality, you just don't.

Some discipline is needed with personal finance. It is very similar to your approach for nutrition.

Everyone enjoys a big meal now and then, but we cannot have a big meal 3 times a day.

That does not work in the long run. It's unhealthy.

PERSONAL FINANCE / SPENDING

RETAIL THERAPY IS A MYTH. Buy what you need. Be smart about it. Have that Starbucks coffee. Buy that new tennis racquet.

Can we agree that you don't need everything today? Prioritize what is important.

Stay on schedule with your expenses or allowances to ensure positive cash flow. That is how you win in personal finance.

Emotional and psychological triggers are traps to increase your impulse purchases. That is by design. We are sure you see all of those advertisements on social media and on TV.

The last three pages were about transforming you into an educated consumer. One that spends with a purpose. One that quickly checks prices. One that does not overpay for convenience. One that respects and values his/her money.

OPPORTUNITY COST

Remember that there is some scarcity to spending your money. You can't spend $20 more than once. Once it is spent, it is gone.

By choosing "Opportunity A", you cannot pursue "Opportunity B".

There is a cost to your decision. You are voting with your money, on every purchase.

Should that money go to a fancier car or just maybe that money should be saved/invested for you?

Should I spend that money today or just maybe I would like to go to that concert in two months?

You cannot have BOTH right now. Maybe tomorrow. Just not today.

PERSONAL FINANCE / SPENDING

POWER 5 SPENDING PRINCIPLES (when in doubt, reference these)

1. Pay yourself 1st, then spend 2nd.
   - Creates immediate cash flow
   - Every income source, use a simpler percentage (10 to 20%)
   - Builds an emergency fund
   - Creates ammo for future opportunities

2. Choose "experiences" over "things".
   - Make new memories
   - Explore nature
   - Enhances self discovery
   - Go see a game or concert, enjoy your life

3. Spend like an educated consumer
   - Research products
   - Avoid emotional or psychological triggers
   - Be patient about bigger purchases

4. Cash over cards
   - Use cash or debit cards exclusively
   - Digital money should only be used online
   - Only use credit cards for small purchases to build credit

5. Prioritize personal values
   - Spend more towards your areas of happiness
   - Spend to explore new hobbies or likes
   - Invest forward on skill sets that can be monetized

PERSONAL FINANCE / FICO

CREDIT SCORE

Your credit score begins the first time you take out a loan or sign up for that dangerous credit card.

Your credit score (FICO) is a number that helps lenders understand how likely you are to repay what you borrowed on time.

Just like in the fixed income markets, the better your credit, the more favorable your financial rates will be (lower interest). It makes a big difference over time.

The FICO system is inverted, the better your rating (higher), the better your borrowing rate (lower).

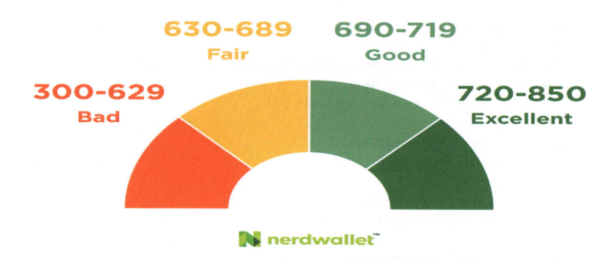

Average Interest Rates by Credit Score

CREDIT SCORE	AVERAGE APR NEW CAR	AVERAGE APR USED CAR
781-850	4.19%	4.69%
661-780	5.01%	6.38%
601-660	7.91%	10.91%
501-600	12.17%	16.78%

Source: Experian: State of the Automotive Finance Market Q4 2018.

PERSONAL FINANCE / FICO

Your FICO score reflects your credit worthiness to the banks. By being responsible, you are saving REAL $$ when financing assets.

The lower rates will help you preserve cash flow. A $50 difference in a monthly payment really adds up over time. We prove this below.

Example: $20000 used car loan below

Average Interest Rates by Credit Score

CREDIT SCORE	AVERAGE APR NEW CAR	AVERAGE APR USED CAR
781-850	4.19%	4.69%
661-780	5.01%	6.38%
601-660	7.91%	10.91%
501-600	12.17%	16.78%

Source: Experian: State of the Automotive Finance Market Q4 2018.

Used Car Loan - FICO Cost Difference
$20k Car, 5 year term

FICO Range	Rate	Monthly Payment	Total Interest Paid
781 - 850	4.69	375	$ 2,475
661 - 780	6.38	390	$ 3,412
601 - 660	10.91	434	$ 6,037
501 - 600	16.78	495	$ 9,681

The green line - Best FICO score, enjoys the cheapest financing rates, has the lowest monthly payment and pays the lowest interest over the five year term.

The gray (bottom) line - Worst FICO score, pays the most expensive financing rates, the highest monthly payment and pays 4 times the amount of interest versus the green line. Do not mess with FICO and pay your bills on time, so you do not overpay for financing like the 501-600 group.

PERSONAL FINANCE / REVIEW

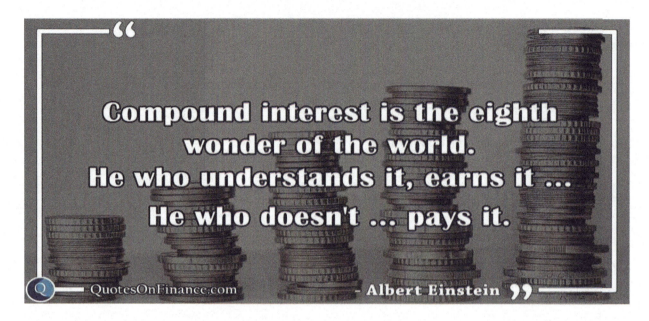

Personal finance begins and ends with your cash flow. Positive cash flow allows you to live your best life. It buys you time and options.

You want to earn compounding returns on your investments.

You can't afford to fight compounding returns on credit card balances.
It is very expensive and an awful way to live.

Build the habit of paying yourself first. This guarantees positive cashflow.
It is simple and young adult friendly.

The FICO system is about financial responsibility. Make sure to pay all your bills on time. A low credit score can affect your job search. Low credit scores create higher borrowing rates, which are costly. You end up overpaying for financing with a low FICO number.

Understand real needs versus wants. You don't need everything today.

We covered the spending approach with our POWER 5 PRINCIPLES. It is a simple guide to help you spend that hard earned money more effectively.

What gets measured, gets improved.

Know your money numbers. Know your money personality. You might need a budget.

FINAL THOUGHTS

I hope you were able to learn something new or interesting about how money works on this journey together.

We live in exciting times with all this new technology. Never before has so much content been so widely available.

Always be learning. That should never stop.

So keep an open mind, a positive outlook and try to keep progressing forward.

Knowledge is everywhere. Learning who you are, what you like and what you are good at is very important.

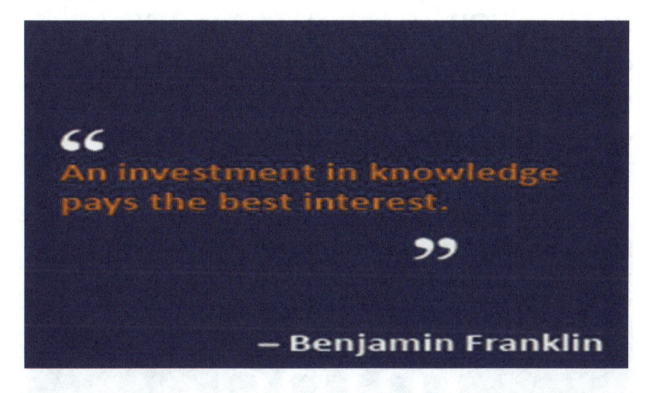

I'm showing you this quote from Benjamin Franklin for a few reasons. He was a brilliant man who also was a Founding Father to our country. He was able to think creatively about solving problems. He invented bi-focal glasses and the early stove.

Does the above quote make sense to you?

Would you have understood this quote as well if you had not taken this journey through Financial Literacy with me?

I hope the answer to the first question is a strong YES.
I also hope that you understand your potential.

Of course, we don't always understand everything the first time. No one cares. Read it again. Come back to it. But keep going. If it matters to you, stay with it. It is worth it.

Trust us.

Financial Knowledge and application are a core life skill. Life is better when your money skills improve. It gets simpler.

Love and respect yourself enough to do the work today for an even better version of yourself tomorrow. That's how Assets become more valuable with time.

Because YOU are in fact, an Asset. Your developing skill sets will determine how much of an Income Producing Asset you will become.

TRUSTED FIN LIT RESOURCES

SECTION SIX
GLOSSARY (REFERENCE)

GLOSSARY (For Your Reference)

Asset: Anything of value that you own. Can be physical, financial or intellectual

Business Cycle: How an Economy can grow or contract and the length of time. There are four phases.

Bitcoin: Digital currency. Technology removed it from Government control. Has a purpose that is not fully known or understood.

Cash Flow: Can be business or personal. Positive cash flow is money remaining after expenses. On the personal side, negative cash flow leads to credit card debt.

Compounding Returns: Financial magic that can work for or against you. The returns of investments left alone grow faster. The debt of credit cards not paid grow faster over time.

Consumer: Those who buy goods or services. We are consumers. Marketing makes us want more than we need. Become a smarter consumer with discipline.

Cost of Goods Sold: Amount of expenses used to create a product or service. We need this to get to NET profits.

Credit: In Fixed Income markets, the better your Credit the lower your rate and interest paid. Same for consumers (FICO).

Credit Card Debt: The unfortunate result of not understanding your cash flow and making impulsive decisions. Adds to stress. Ruins marriages. Just not worth it.

Customers: They pay Gross prices. They are the consumers to your business.

Deflation: Prices are contracting in an Economy based on a basket of goods. Dangerous because demand for things slows down.

Demand: How much Consumers want to buy a product. It's very similar to popularity. It's the level of interest at price.

Expenses: What a consumer pays for things to survive. Can be fixed or variable. Mortgages are fixed. Going to dinner is variable.

Fiat Currency: Backed by Governments. Examples are the US$, the Euro, and the Japanese Yen.

FICO Score: Ranking system that rewards being responsible about paying your bills, credit cards and loans on time. The higher the number the better. Good score means lower rate, less interest paid out.

Financial Assets: Cash, Stocks, Bonds, Currency, Commodities and Real Estate. You want them to become more valuable.

Gross Profits: What your customers pay for your goods or services. Does not include the costs or expenses involved in the sale.

Inflation: Prices are increasing on a basket of goods in an Economy. This is normal and expected in a growing economy. Interest Rates paid to banks include some Inflation in the rate. Investments need to outpace Inflation over time for true wealth creation

Literacy: Ability to read or write. Can also mean knowledge.

Money: The first financial asset. Created the ability to buy or sell rather than exchange. Can be coin, paper or digital. Just a tool.

Needs: Food, shelter, water and clothing. Should also include a stable and supportive environment.

Net Profits: Profits that remain after including COGS or expenses involved in the sale of a company's good or services.

Nominal Interest Rate: Rates paid by both Corps and Consumers to borrow money or finance assets. Has two components, the real interest rates + inflation rate.

Opportunity Cost: By buying something for a certain amount, you can't buy something different with that amount. You can only spend a given $20 bill once.

Real Interest Rate: Consider the true rate because Inflation is removed. Mostly academic.

Risk: Knowing that not everything is guaranteed. That you can lose part of your investment sometimes. They are known and unknown.
Prices can go up or down for many reasons.

Supply: Amount of a product available for sale. Too much supply without enough demand causes lower prices.

Sub-Contracting: Scheduling the work while other people do the job for you. Part of our babysitting example.

Wants: What the marketing people make you think you should buy or do to be happy. They are rewards. Don't always have to have it.

The End.

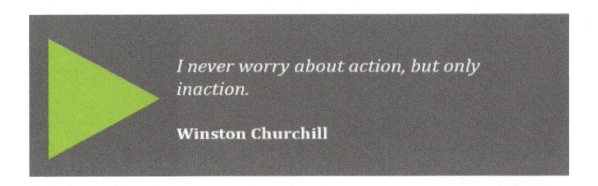

Contact Us:

Jon Bloom

coachjonbloom@gmail.com

@Bloomlifeskills (Twitter)

Paul Richmond

prichmond53@gmail.com

@TheCoachRich (Twitter)

Looking forward to hearing from you!

Notes:

Crypto Literacy for Newbies (Bonus Material)

@Bloomlifeskills (twitter)

Crypto Literacy for Newbies
@Bloomlifeskills (twitter)

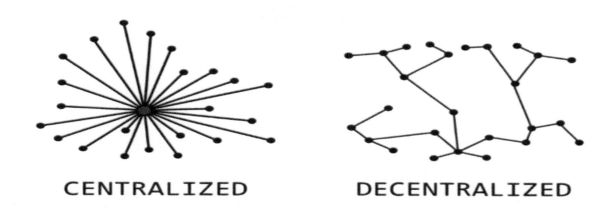

What is Crypto-Currency?

I think the most important distinction for crypto currency is that it is not backed by the strength/weakness of a country's economy or military (Fiat). Nations will never be able to fully control or kill it off. Collective computers across the global internet run the code. Countries can ban it but they will only be left behind. The Crypto Space continues to evolve rapidly. It's important to remember that we will continue to see this new digital technology mainstream into our lives over the next 5 to 10 years.

The original design might have been for peer to peer payments. Bitcoin has evolved into more of a store of wealth now. We are seeing more direct technology applications being built than ever across the crypto ecosystem.

Crypto is not fully regulated yet, which does create a bigger opportunity for those who properly DYOR. DYOR simply means to do your own research. Crypto enables direct financial transactions between end users. It also allows end users to enter into contracts without any intermediation (third party between).

Crypto Market Stats:

There are currently 16k crypto currencies available now to the public. The full value of all these coins are roughly $2.1T (Trillion) as I write this guide. Bitcoin is approximately 38% of the entire market. Ethereum is roughly 18% of the entire market. Bitcoin and Ethereum are the dominant market players. The remaining 44% of the crypto market are all considered alt coins.

Just like the early days of the internet, you must consider that the majority of coins/tokens will not survive long term. Maybe 200 to 300 of the 16k are legitimate and deserve to make it.

Percentage wise, that means maybe 2-3% of the total coins/tokens will actually survive the long term. There must be a utility case for a coin or token to survive. This guide will attempt to help you identify those with true promise.

The History of Crypto:

Just because a currency is digital does not mean that it is actually a crypto currency. So, we need to review some history. I'll make it short and sweet like usual.

Before Bitcoin: There's a reason why people don't carry around thousands of dollars in their physical wallets. It's dangerous. It's risky. So, the early attempts were just about avoiding physical money for security reasons. The concept of a decentralized blockchain did not exist either yet. Here are some examples of electronic cash that existed before Bitcoin hit our timeline. Again, these were not crypto.

- DigiCash
- PayPal
- Bmoney
- HashCash

Bitcoin Arrives: The White paper goes public on 10/31/2008. The first block (Genesis) was created on 1/3/2009.

We now have internet money. We now have a shared open ledger where everyone can see every transaction, ever made. Eventually people begin to realize they should hold Bitcoin rather than spend it. Bitcoin becomes accepted as a tremendous store of value. It's accepted as a powerful hedge against weakening fiat money. Bitcoin is now just 13 years old. Think about that please. We are all still so early!

Ethereum: Genesis Block 7/30/2015
Anything other than Bitcoin is technically an Altcoin. Yes, there were other Alts before Ethereum. But in all fairness..they don't really matter..right now. Ethereum is so young and is the predominant blockchain that crypto projects are either built on or will be built on.

What are Blockchains?

Nobody owns the blockchain infrastructure directly. Instead many computers across the globe carry the same code and chains on all of them. These computers validate every single transaction. To destroy a chain you would need to control 51% of the global computers at the same damn time. Is that really possible?

A blockchain is a distributed database that is shared among the nodes across the entire network. As a database, a blockchain stores information electronically in digital format.

Blockchains are best known for their crucial role in cryptocurrency systems, such as Bitcoin, for maintaining a secure and decentralized record of transactions. The innovation with a blockchain is that it guarantees the fidelity and security of a record of data and generates trust without the need for a trusted third party,

One key difference between a typical database and a blockchain is how the data is structured. A blockchain collects information together in groups, known as blocks, that hold sets of information. Blocks have certain storage capacities and, when filled, are closed and linked to the previously filled block, forming a chain of data known as the blockchain. All new information that follows that freshly added block is compiled into a newly formed block that will then also be added to the chain once filled.

Consensus Mechanisms / Proof of What Exactly?

Consensus mechanisms are how all participating nodes come into agreement about the true and valid state of the blockchain network. This ensures the right transactions are confirmed and recorded on the blockchain. It also helps avoid erroneous transactions which we call "double spend". Now let's discuss the big 3:

Proof of Work (PoW) In PoW, miners have to solve a cryptographic puzzle to validate a transaction. One might visualize it as a race, where the miners are competing to be the first one to solve the puzzle. The answer to this race/puzzle is known as a hash.

- Nodes are Miners
- Computing power matters
- Miners produce coins, they receive rewards
- Significant energy consuming process
- Highest quality of Decentralization

Proof of Stake (PoS) In PoS, computational power is replaced by currency power. It depends on the number of tokens a node has in its pool. In other words, your ability to validate a transaction depends on how much "stake" you have in the network. This consensus does not mine coins. Some projects start off in PoW and then move to PoS. Ethereum is in the process of shifting to PoS.

- Nodes are Validators
- Size of staking pools matters
- No coins are produced in PoS
- Validators receive the fees
- Lowest quality of Decentralization

 vs.

To add each block to the chain, miners must compete to solve a difficult puzzle using their computers processing power.

There is no competition as the block creator is chosen by an algorithm based on the user's stake.

In order to add a malicious block, you'd have to have a computer more powerful than 51% of the network.

In order to add a malicious block, you'd have to own 51% of all the cryptocurrency on the network.

The first miner to solve the puzzle is given a reward for their work.

There is no reward for making a block, so the block creator takes a transaction fee.

Proof of Burn (POB) Proof-of-Burn uses virtual mining rigs instead of physical ones to validate transactions. Virtual PoB miners initiate coin burns as a way to show their involvement in the network and be allowed to mine. Computing power matters here like PoW. Coins are burnt by sending them to dead addresses. Dead addresses do not have private keys. They cannot ever be used. Dead addresses lower public supply. It's the crypto version of stock buybacks.

- Nodes are Virtual Miners
- Computing power matters
- Miners produce coins into dead wallets
- Significant energy consuming process
- Medium quality of Decentralization

Tokens vs. Coins

Just a quick clarification here..

Coins have their own native blockchain. They operate independently of any other platform.

Tokens are built on other blockchains. They are built on top of an already existing blockchain. Meme coins are actually tokens. Stable coins are actually tokens.

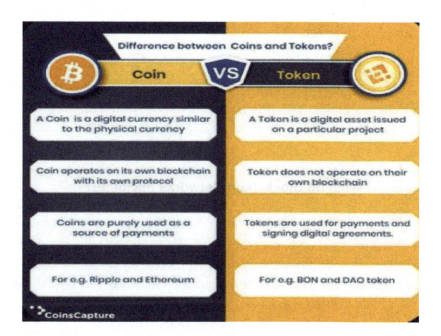

Tokenomics / DYOR

This is a very important section so listen up. We will now discuss some factors around the coins/tokens that will determine the level of public demand. The degree of demand vs. supply will determine current and projected market capitalizations.

Leadership Team: Are they reputable? Have they worked on any other already successful crypto projects? We really like to see that. We want dependable people that will execute the plan.

Use Case: What problem does this project solve? How does it benefit other coins/tokens now and in the future? Does it save money? Does it help with transaction speed? Are there social benefits? Stuff like that

Distribution: How was the initial supply released? What's the current public supply? What amount will max supply look like at maturity? Was it all done in a fair manner?

Production: How are these new coins/tokens being created? Which consensus algorithm are they using?

Community: Each project has a community. What are they like? Why are they in the project? Do they only care about making money or is there a greater purpose? Are they inclusive? Are they trying to improve any social issues?

Inflationary or Deflationary: If more coins are being created than are being burned the project will be inflationary. If more coins are being burned than created, we are then in a deflationary state. Deflationary states are good because total public supply is being reduced over time. And that will increase the value per coin.

Summary: When you are able to find a project with a strong leadership team. A project that has actually solves something (utility) important for Crypto..with good tokenomics and a great community. You will have a project with true upside potential. Community alone will not get you there. The top coins and some tokens check most of these boxes.

What do Blockchain Networks Facilitate?

Blockchains allow digital information to be recorded and distributed. Because they cannot be edited after the fact, we can trust the outcomes. Records cannot be deleted, altered or destroyed. The many nodes carrying the network across the globe guarantee that.

Smart Contracts - Computer code that can be built into the blockchain to facilitate, verify, or negotiate a contract agreement. Smart contracts operate under a set of conditions to which users agree. When those conditions are met, the terms of the agreement are then carried out.

Non-Fungible Tokens - NFTs are cryptographic assets on a blockchain with unique identification codes and metadata that does distinguish them from one another. Unlike other crypto, they cannot be traded or exchanged at equivalency. This differs from fungible tokens like cryptocurrencies, which are identical to each other. NFTs are like unique swaps. They are custom fit. They are absolutely unique.

NFTs are similar to meme coins because they both derive a healthy part of their value from their community size and strength. NFTs are about the artwork right now. NFTs will evolve more into legal and financial contracts going forward. NFTs will be the results of an executed smart contract most likely.

Layer 2 - The Bridges/The Connectors

Layer 2 is a secondary protocol built on top of an existing blockchain. They help scale the larger blockchains that are having traffic issues. The L2s can process some of the information away from the main nets. They are mostly tokens.

Optimistic Rollups: All transactions are considered valid here on the main net. They get involved post transaction. They help reduce gas cost by running calculations away from the main net.

The name 'Optimistic Rollup' refers to how 'optimistic' aggregators tend to run without committing fraud and instead provide proofs in case of fraud, while 'rollup' is from the process of implementing transaction bundles that are 'rolled up' and that thus allow network transaction speeds to increase exponentially.

Zero Knowledge Rollups: These process bundles of information with a focus on validity. Also known as a ZK Rollup or ZKR — is a Layer-2 scaling solution that uses zk-SNARKs (privacy-based cryptographic proofs) to allow blockchains to bundle transactions into one computation prior to execution by using a smart contract. Sometimes used in unison with decentralized exchange (DEX) protocols, implementing zk-Rollups on some blockchains can lead to lower transaction fees, improved liquidity, enhanced non-custodial crypto ownership, and more.

Metaverse

The Metaverse is a combination of multiple elements made up of technology, including virtual reality, augmented reality and video.

Users get to "live" within a digital universe. Its a plural term because it will be a combination of worlds and even perhaps dimensions. This is still a very young sector with tremendous potential. The VR in our house is really popular. Ready Play One is a great movie to get some exposure to what the Metaverse could become one day.

DeFi (Decentralized Finance)

Decentralized finance or DeFi is the new financial system built on blockchains. Its peer-to-peer financial transactions being conducted away from the banking system or wall street. There are fewer tolls and rents to pay along the way here. It's the continuation of online banking without the bank.

Various financial transactions are now possible with DeFi's 'smart contracts' that execute financial transactions under certain conditions.

There are many different decentralized applications, or dApps, and uses within DeFi that open more accessibility and features. But they all come with additional risk. A strong community can help you find safer and vetted projects.

This sector is still young, still not 100% safe enough..so pls be careful about WHERE and HOW you transact. There are still many little manual steps needed to get the crypto and money where it needs to be. Go slow and be careful please.

DeFI staking, in its most narrow definition, refers to the practice of locking crypto assets into a smart contract in exchange for becoming a validator in a DeFi protocol or a L1 blockchain. The stakers earn rewards back to applying their crypto value to the project. In essence when you stake you are helping fund their project.

Yield Farming: One of the biggest challenges DeFi protocols face is attracting new liquidity. DeFi needs deep liquidity for liquidity pools to work, which is why the landscape can be so competitive. So growing projects will offer substantial returns for your participation. Just know that these opportunities are most likely shorter term and that you may be at risk in price per token as well.

DeFi implies self-custody. You should know your private key and should also have moved your positions off the larger CEX's.

Play to Earn / GameFi

Users play games built on the blockchain, but they earn real monetary rewards as they progress. What primarily differentiates them from traditional games is that players play to earn rewards that can be used in real life.

Imagine playing online Monopoly, but you get to keep some of the money from winning. This is another emerging, younger sector in crypto with massive upside. People love to play games that provide rewards back when achievements or levels are unlocked. We are all trained for that now.

Web 3.0

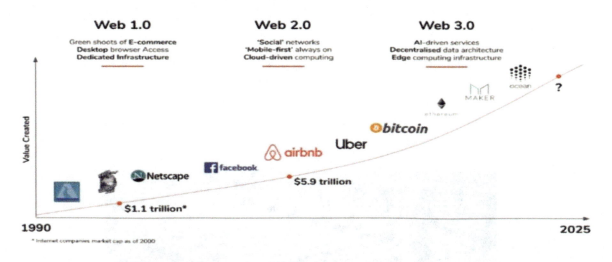

This is a fun subject. There is plenty of speculation about Web3 these days. We are not quite there yet. Web 3 is still being built out. We do expect it to be more decentralized than Web2.

Web3 will be powered by multiple blockchains. Web3 will make some centralizing platforms obsolete. I anticipate that Web3 will have better mental health benefits depending on the level of influence platforms will still have. In web3, users will have more control over their own data. More wealth will stick with the end users.

Web 3 is not the metaverse. Web 3 just means that the future of the internet is just more decentralized. Most people won't even know or care. But early Investors will do well to watch as this continues to play out.

The Macro of it all

Today I consider crypto to be a sub asset of currency. Bitcoin which was originally intended for peer-to-peer payments but has now evolved into an optimal asset to store value. So, Bitcoin has digital gold properties. And gold is a hard commodity. Defi will continue to challenge the Fixed Income markets. Especially for smaller size transactions. And finally there is so much digital technology being built in crypto..it would be foolish not to consider that one day crypto projects will challenge some more stock valuations.

To recap, crypto has the potential to disrupt ALL the asset classes as the space matures. Technology has always removed layers, and we can expect that to keep happening behind blockchain..which is crypto as well.

Mining (PoW)

"Mining" is performed using sophisticated hardware that solves an extremely complex computational math problem. The first computer to find the solution to the problem is awarded the next block of crypto. The process of competition then begins anew. Over and over again.

Miners buy their own equipment. Miners pay their own electricity costs. Miners hope to "out earn" both their initial costs and their monthly utility costs. It definitely works. When done properly crypto mining is a nice passive income stream. We are fans.

When you earn/produce more Income than your sunken cost and utility bill..then mining becomes a nice passive income. Not before.

Meme Tokens

Hear me out please. Sometimes the joke becomes reality. Because meme coins are actually tokens because they don't have their blockchains. Most people already know about Doge. Now most people are hearing about Shiba. Internet memes are very powerful in branding. Meme tokens bring new people into Crypto. So do NFTs.

Some memes do reach legitimate market capitalization based on their popularity. The higher market cap meme tokens have incredibly strong communities. And to their credit some Meme Tokens are actually adding some utility around them.

Meme coins have great communities behind them. But we must be aware that most of these don't have any actual use case that helps anything. That's a problem. So be careful and maybe just avoid them. The pump and dump risk is very high here. There better be a team behind it. The Devs better be working 24/7. You have to really DYOR here. It's so risky.

Avoiding Scams

There are so many scams in crypto because of the tremendous upside in this space. The future growth is juicy. So the thieves are plenty. They are sophisticated in earning your trust, or with elegant deception. Whatever it takes to separate you from your NFT or coins, they have set up the traps for it to happen today.

Discord: Don't answer dms from people you don't know on discord. They are not giving you anything. Sorry but you are not that lucky.

Fake Websites: You see a reward. It takes you to a slick website. They get your wallet info. Boom, your coins are gone. Slow down. Protect your neck. Again people don't give away bitcoin.

Give to get more: A fake twitter account with a picture of Elon Musk wants to give your crypto. The only catch is that you have to give them yours first. Do you? Heck no you don't. You have to be street smart about sharing any information publicly.

Where to Trade

We are comfortable recommending the following centralized exchanges to begin your crypto journey:

Coinbase: https://bit.ly/31EUEnG

Kucoin: https://m.kucoin.com/

Voyager: https://bit.ly/3HPnsJK

How to Secure Your Positions

POV: You are a proud newbie owner of your 1st crypto position. Now what?

You will need a wallet at some point. Especially for DeFi.

A crypto wallet is a software program designed to store both your public and private keys. You can then send and receive digital currencies in/out. You can also monitor and track your balances in each coin. You will need a wallet to manage your crypto holdings. Especially because you want to keep them secure.

Private Key: For your eyes only. Do not share with anyone. This is your recovery code.

Public Key: This key is for receiving/sending crypto. The public key is safe to use when moving a position off the centralized exchanges. The public key is also used for NFTs and in DeFi when needed.

If you don't know your keys, then you don't truly own your coin. They are still centralized. You may own them, but you don't have control over them.

How do you like your wallets? Hot or Cold?

Hot Wallets are connected to the Internet. They are cloud wallets; they are mobile wallets. They are software wallets, and they are also the central exchange wallets (CEX). These are for ST holds.

Cold Wallets are offline. They are hardware. They are even written on paper. These are for LT holds.

General Security Tips:

Unfortunately, the Crypto space has a lot of bad people trying to use their malicious software to acquire your bags. It is really bad out there. And because we are still in early stages, the ecosystem puts all the responsibility on the end user. Take your time when copying and moving positions. Embrace your pc security. Use 2FA when possible. Acute awareness is key on the security side.

Avoiding Scams

Unfortunately, you must be super careful with Crypto. It has some value today. It will have more value tomorrow. The money movements are digital. So, we have bad actors all over the world just looking to hack your bags.

So be street smart about everything you do.

Discord DMs - If you don't know the person from your community. Just block, don't even open.

Give to Get - Don't ever send anyone any of your crypto, you won't ever get back more. Elon isn't giving you any crypto. Nobody else will either.

Fake Accounts - Hackers will pretend to be someone else. And then they ask about your trading. Then they connect to your wallet or get you on their fake website.

Hype - Influencers get airdrops of coins. In exchange they promote said coin. Don't ever buy something just because a famous Tik Toker jumped in. Do the research please. Ask for help.

Where to Research

Coin Gecko: Is one of my favorite crypto apps. You can find out where to buy the coin/token. You can get some history on it. You can get a lot of important statistics. It's easily my go to at the beginning of the research process.   Link here: https://bit.ly/338U9mg

I also have a watchlist of names to keep an eye on.

I think the Crypto community does a great job on Spaces too. You can find some amazing information just by listening in.

Be careful who you listen to online though. The right people are positioning you for the medium to long term. They are professional. They most likely are not on Tik Tok. Avoid the traders and the influencers that pressure or rush you into something.

Glossary of Terms:

General Search: https://bit.ly/3zyan4F

Blockchain: https://bit.ly/3n6GOSx

Centralization: https://bit.ly/3JNbyIp

CeFi: https://bit.ly/3zEB1IX

Consensus Algorithms: https://bit.ly/3G8g9fA

DAO: https://bit.ly/3n7pkp7

DeFi: https://bit.ly/3qWQpwp

Digital Identity: https://bit.ly/3f2MzMM

Drawdowns: https://bit.ly/3eXwrw5

FOMO: https://bit.ly/3HHiChB

FUD: https://bit.ly/32YN3kr

Genesis Block: https://bit.ly/32Zez1p

Interoperability: https://bit.ly/3n424Z2

Market Capitalization: https://bit.ly/3JQxoVe

Metaverse: https://bit.ly/3qWUwsl

Mining: https://bit.ly/3HL9W9O

Nodes: https://bit.ly/3zCWJxd

Protocols: https://bit.ly/3n4T3iB

Volatility: https://bit.ly/3t3XKwL

Wallet: https://bit.ly/3qQRB4g

Crypto Resources

Wikipedia/Bitcoin: https://en.wikipedia.org/wiki/Bitcoin

Satoshi Whitepaper: https://bitcoin.org/bitcoin.pdf

Cryptopedia Glossary: https://www.gemini.com/learn/glossary

Great write-up on Web3 & The Metaverse: https://bit.ly/32NmcHA

Crypto Security & Safety: https://bit.ly/3eDoETV

Coinbase Link:: https://bit.ly/34jcCwV (affiliate link)

What is the Metaverse: https://www.wired.com/story/what-is-the-metaverse/

Binance Academy: https://academy.binance.com/en

Next Steps

- **Rate the guide on Gumroad please**
- **Follow @Bloomlifeskills on twitter**
- **Tell you friends online & IRL about this free resource**

Stay safe and good luck y'all

@Bloomlifeskills (twitter)

Made in the USA
Monee, IL
14 October 2022